JUPITER HAMMON

32

AN

ADDRESS

TO THE

NEGROES

In the STATE of NEW-YORK,

By JUPITER HAMMON,

Servant of JOHN LLOYD, jun, Esq; of the Manor of
Queen's Village, Long-Island.

"Of a truth I perceive that God is no respecter of
"persons:
"But in every Nation, he that feareth him and
"worketh righteousness, is accepted with him."—
Acts x. 34. 35.

NEW-YORK:

Printed by CARROLL and PATTERSON
No. 32, Maiden-Lane.

M,DCC,LXXXVII.

JUPITER HAMMON
AMERICAN NEGRO POET

SELECTIONS FROM HIS WRITINGS
AND A
BIBLIOGRAPHY

By
OSCAR WEGELIN

The Black Heritage Library Collection

 BOOKS FOR LIBRARIES PRESS
FREEPORT, NEW YORK

First Published 1915

Reprinted 1969

Second Reprinting 1970

Reprinted from a copy in the
Fisk University Library Negro Collection

INTERNATIONAL STANDARD BOOK NUMBER:
0-8369-8682-2

LIBRARY OF CONGRESS CATALOG CARD NUMBER:
70-83900

PRINTED IN THE UNITED STATES OF AMERICA

John Nelson Lloyd

Nº 14

Jno. N. Lloyd.

JUPITER HAMMON

"My old negroes are to be provided for."
With these words ends the codicil to the will of
Henry Lloyd, owner and lord of Lloyd's Neck,
or Queen's Village, dated March 3, 1763.

While these words convey nothing of especial
interest in themselves, they are to the student
of American literature of paramount import-
ance as among the "old negroes" was a man, a
slave, who was destined to become, nay, had
already become the first one of his race to see
his name in print as a writer of verse in what
we are now pleased to call the United States of
America.

For without doubt, Jupiter Hammon, the
subject of this volume, was the first member
of the negro race to write and publish poetry
in this country. For more than a century
Phillis Wheatley has been lauded throughout
the English-speaking world as the first of her
race to appear in print as a versifier, at least
so far as America was concerned. It will be
shown however in this sketch of Hammon that
not only did he antedate Miss Wheatley by nearly ten years as a poet, but at least one of his
poems was printed before she had reached these
shores, or knew one word of English.

The earliest trace of Hammon is found in a

7

letter dated 1730 when the poet must have been a child of ten or twelve years. I give it in full, as follows:

"St. Georges May 19 1730

Sir: I'm informed by Mr Lloyd Jupiter is afflicted wth pains in his Leggs Knees and thighs ascending to his bowels wch in my Esteem is a gouty Rumatick Disorder to releave which and Prevent the Impending Danger (as you observe) of its getting up to his Stomach, Desire the following Directions may be vsed. In the first place give one of the Purges, In the morning fasting, and all night one of the boluses, the next day take away about 12 or 14 ounces of blood (notwithstanding he loost blood in the winter) from the foot will be the most serviceable a day or two after as you find his strength will bear it, give the other purge, and the bolus att night, on those days he doth not purge and is bled give one of the powdrs in the Morning and another in the Evening mixt in some Diet Drink made to the equal of Horse Reddish Roots the bark of elder Root Pine Budds or the second bark wood or Toad sorrel, make it stronger with the Ingredients and Lett him drink constantly of it for a month or six weeks and then the remainder of the summer let him have milch whey to drink he must live on a thin spare diet abstaining from meat att nights all spiritous liquors salt pepper and vinegar have sent some oyntmt to be used as he did the former

with my affectionate Regard^s

to Vncle and Aunt best Respects to all yr good family I Remain

Your Most Humble and Obed^t serv^t

G. MUIRSON."

8

Nearly twenty years ago the late Daniel Parish, Jr., told the writer that he had in his collection a broadside poem written by Hammon which was earlier than anything that had been written by a negro in America, as far as could be traced. He had, however, mislaid it and could not recall its title. As his statement seemed so remarkable, I at first doubted its correctness, but as this gentleman was well known as an expert among students of Early American Poetry, I still hoped that what he said would some day be proven. Until his death, which occurred in December of last year, Mr. Parish was unable to find this elusive broadside, and it seemed that it must be forever lost and the point that I had tried to prove would be forever unsolved. Whenever this "supposed" broadside was mentioned to any of the delvers into the literature of the Colonial period, my surmises regarding Hammon's priority as a poet were received with grave doubt.

I, however, had faith in the statement made by the departed collector and when a few months ago Mr. Chas. Fred. Heartman issued his admirable bibliography of Miss Wheatley, I determined to endeavor once more to locate the long lost broadsheet. With this end in view I wrote to Mr. Robert H. Kelby, Librarian of the

New York Historical Society, and inquired of that gentleman if perchance he had discovered among a collection of pamphlets relating to slavery which Mr. Parish had, prior to his death, presented to the society, a broadside poem by one Jupiter Hammon. I described the piece as well as I knew how, expecting that a search would have to be made among a large lot of material. Imagine my surprise when almost immediately I received a reply stating that the broadside that I had been searching for for years was not in the lot of pamphlets presented by Mr. Parish, but was in its proper place among the broadsides belonging to the Society's collection, where it had evidently been for many years.

This was certainly good news, as it proved peradventure that my surmise had been correct, and that Miss Wheatley would have to step down from the pedestal she had so long occupied.

My ambition, however, in making this discovery was not to dethrone the dusky versifier of Boston, but I wanted to do justice to one who almost unknown, yet must have been a man of considerable ability and of influence among the members of his own race, bondman though he had been.

Unfortunately, none of his contemporaries

2 *

AN
Evening's Improvement.

SHEWING,

The NECESSITY of beholding
the LAMB of GOD.

To which is added,

A DIALOGUE;

ENTITLED,

The KIND MASTER and
DUTIFUL SERVANT.

Written by JUPITER HAMMON, a Negro
Man belonging to Mr. *John Lloyd,* of Queen's
Village, on Long-Island, now in Hartford.

HARTFORD:

Printed for the Author, by the Assistance of his Friends.

seemed to have left behind anything which would throw any light upon his life, in fact the only thing that is known of this interesting character is gathered from his own statements that appear in the most popular of his writings, *An Address to the Negroes of the State of New York*. In this address, which exhorts the slaves to be true to their masters, he writes, "When I was in Hartford in Connecticut, where I lived during the War, I published several pieces which were well received, not only by those of my own colour, but by a number of the White people, who thought they might do good among their servants. This is one consideration, among others, that emboldens me now to publish what I have written to you. . . . I am now upwards of seventy years old." This would make the date of his birth about 1720. Where he first saw the light of day, I am unable to state, in fact, were his birth place in Africa, or more probable, the West Indies, he himself was without doubt unable to give the exact date of his natal day. (The letter of Muirson seems to prove that he was born in this country.)

From the tenor of his writings, both Poetical and Prose, I am inclined to believe with Mr. A. A. Schomburg, that Hammon was a preacher among his people. Mr. Schomburg is almost certain that he preached or led religious gatherings, in Hartford and New Haven. His presence in Hartford during the period of the Revolutionary War is explained by the fact that his master, Joseph Lloyd, was a patriot and was compelled to forsake Long Island when the British and Hessians overran it.

The poem which establishes Hammon's priority as an American Negro versifier, is entitled, "An Evening Thought. Salvation by Christ, with Penetential Cries: Composed by Jupiter Hammon, a Negro belonging to Mr. Lloyd, of Queen's Village, on Long Island, the 25th of December, 1760." It is a broadside, evidently printed at New York early in the following year. The poem comprises 88 lines printed in double column.

Hammon was evidently much interested in Salvation as that word appears no less than twenty-three times in this poem. This slave served no less than three members of the Lloyd Family. At the time that this poem was written he was owned by Henry Lloyd, whom he served until the latter's death, which occurred in 1763. (I have mentioned the clause in his will which directed that his negroes should be cared for.) At his death he left the Neck to his four sons, but Hammon became the property of Joseph, who when the British overran the Island fled to Connecticut. Joseph died during the War and left his part of the Neck to John Lloyd, Jr. This John, who was a grandson of Joseph, became the last owner of Hammon, who at this time was a man of about 60 years of age.

His second publication was a poetical address to Phillis Wheatley, dated "Hartford, August 4, 1778." It is also printed in broadsheet form, and only one copy is known to exist.

His next appearance in print was entitled, "An essay on the Ten Virgins." This was issued at Hartford the following year. I have been unable to locate a copy, but it was advertised as "To be sold" in *The Connecticut Courant,* Dec. 14, 1779.

Nothing now appeared from his pen until 1782, when Hudson & Goodwin printed at Hartford, "A Winter Piece." This was largely in prose, but contained on the last two pages, "A Poem for Children with thoughts on Death."

Hammon was evidently much taken up with thoughts on death, and in his Address to the Negroes he writes, "If we should ever get to Heaven, we shall find nobody to reproach us for being black, or for being slaves." Why the if?

His next appearance in print was a religious dissertation which he called "An Evening's Improvement." It was printed at Hartford, probably by Hudson & Goodwin, without date, but undoubtedly during the War. It contains a poetical dialogue, entitled, "The Kind Master and Dutiful Servant."

Hammon's masters were evidently kind to him, probably realizing that he was a slave of more than usual intelligence. As will be seen by referring to the list of his writings at the end of this volume, his friends, among whom were undoubtedly some of the members of the Lloyd family, were of assistance to the author in bringing his writings before the public. Without this help, it is doubtful if any of his writings should have seen the light of day, as Hammon was not well enough known to have publishers as anxious to print his writings, as they were, to issue the poems of Phillis Wheatley. While the latter's writings have been issued in many editions, not only in America, but in Europe as well, those of the Long Island slave never reached beyond a single edition, with the ex-. ception of the "Address to the Negroes," of which as many as three editions were printed, one after the writer's decease.

Hammon's most important work, probably his last, was not in verse, but was an Address to the Negroes of the state in which he dwelt. Its influence was, however, felt beyond the borders of New York, and we find an edition printed in Philadelphia by Daniel Humphreys the year in which the first made its appearance from the press of Carroll and Patterson. This was in 1787. An edition was also printed in New York, 1806, after the author had ceased to be a slave, and (let us hope) had found rest for his soul in that Heaven he had longed for so often and about which he had written his best lines.

A receipt for money which mentions Hammon is in the New York Historical Society and proves that he was living as late as 1790. I herewith give a copy of it.

"Oysterbay 6th Oct 1790 Recd of John Lloyd Junr twelve Pound in full of the last years Interest on his bond Recd by the hand of Jupiter Hammon & have endorsed it on the Bond

P   LORETTA COCK"

£12-0-0

The year of his death is unknown, but it was between the years 1790 and 1806. In the edition of the Address to the Negroes issued in 1806 three residents of Oyster Bay, Long Island, attest over their own signatures that Hammon was a man of good parts and an esteemed neighbor. The publishers of the 1787 edition state that "They have made no material alterations in it, except in the spelling, which they found needed considerable correction." By this it will be seen that Hammon was evidently a man without education. How different a career compared with that of Miss Wheatley, who had the

15

advantages of a good schooling. He, a slave faithfully serving both his Heavenly and earthly Masters, probably almost unknown outside of a small circle in which he moved, while she the child of fortune was petted by all with whom she came in contact. Only an accident prevented her from being introduced to the King of England, George the Third, and the father of his country honored her by sending her an autograph letter.

A few years later, however, she died, broken in spirit, and almost friendless, her later days being darkened through an unfortunate marriage. Her husband, although a man of talent, could not appreciate the gentle and kindly being he had sworn to protect. The portrait affixed to the first edition of her poems shows a face marked with kindness and trust in others. What would we not give to obtain a likeness of "The Negro Servant of John Lloyd, Jr., of Queen's Village."

Several specimens of the hand-writing of Miss Wheatley are known to exist, but nothing in the chirography of Hammon has been found. Were it not for his printed pamphlets and broadsides his very name would now be forgotten and the first of his race to write verse in America would have none to do him honor. Hammon was, however, the earliest negro versifier and a not unworthy forerunner of a numerous company of Afro-American poets, the best of whom was the lamented Paul Lawrence Dunbar.

In two respects both Hammon and Miss Wheatley were alike. They were both of a deeply religious temperament, and both tried to instill their belief into others. How far they succeeded is not for us to decide, but it seems probable that the exhortations of Hammon to his fellow slaves did meet with success. At any rate his white neighbors seemed pleased with his efforts and did what they could to help him.

Although Hammon must have been well known to some of his contemporaries, he is almost totally neglected by biographers and bibliographers. Nor is he mentioned in any of the histories of Long Island. The only notices I have found regarding him, beyond the mere mention of his name, are the following:

"Jupiter Hammon, a Negro Slave of Long Island, attained to considerable advancement, both in an intellectual and religious point of view. He published an address to the negroes of New York, which contains much excellent advice, embodied in language so excellent, that were it not well attested, its genuiness might be justly questioned." Armisted. "A Tribute to the Negro," Manchester, 1848.

"Joseph (Lloyd) had a negro slave, Jupiter

Hammon, who was quite a literary character, and published at Hartford, Dec. '79 an Essay on the Parable of the Ten Virgins." Onderdonk. "Revolutionary Incidents of Queens Co."

The present writer contributed an article on Hammon in the *Literary Collector* for August, 1904. It was headed, "Was Phillis Wheatley America's First Negro Poet?"

Several books relating to the Lloyd Family have been published, one at least by a member of the Family, but not even the name of the slave-poet is mentioned in either of them. Fate seemed anxious to consign him to oblivion, but thanks to the indefatigable searcher for books who first called my attention to the fact that such a man once lived, I am now enabled to place these facts, meagre though they be, before the public. It seems probable that Hammon was the author of more poetry than has been unearthed, but after a diligent search through many of the important public and private libraries of the United States those noted in the bibliography at the end of this volume are all that could be discovered. If there were more, they, like "An Evening Thought" and "An Address to Phillis Wheatley," were probably issued in broadsheet form and have long since vanished. Happily, however, the broadside which furnishes proof of his priority as a poet of colour exists in the single copy now in the New York Historical Society.

In the bibliography I have noted the whereabouts of copies that could be located. In the gathering of the material which made this book possible, imperfect though it may be, I have received valuable assistance from the librarians of the New York Historical Society, the American Antiquarian Society, the John Carter Brown Library, the Massachusetts Historical Society, the New York Public Library, the Long Island Historical Society, the Boston Public Library, and Harvard College Library. Especially am I grateful for assistance rendered by Messrs. Robert H. Kelby, Librarian of the New York Historical Society; Albert C. Bates, Librarian of the Connecticut Historical Society; Orville B. Ackerly, who furnished me with the copy of the Lloyd will of 1763, and Mr. Arthur A. Schomburg, who spent much time in seeking information in some of the libraries of the Nutmeg State.

HAMMON AS A POET

As a poet Hammon will certainly not rank among the "Immortals." His verse is stilted, and while some of his rhymings are fairly even, we can easily comprehend that they were written by one not well versed in the art of poesy.

They have a sameness which is wearying to the reader and there is too much reiteration, in some cases the same or nearly the same words being employed again and again.

His verse is saturated with a religious feeling not always well expressed, as he did not possess the ability to use the right word at the proper time. Hammon was undoubtedly deeply religious, but his religion was somewhat tinged with narrowness and superstition, a not uncommon fault of the time in which he lived and wrote.

Although grammatically almost perfect, it seems certain that an abler and more experienced hand than his own was responsible for this.

Compared with the verses of Phillis Wheatley, his lines are commonplace and few would care to read them more than once. When we consider, however, that this poor slave had probably no other learning than what he had been enabled to secure for himself during his hours of relaxation from labor, it is surprising that the results are not more meagre. Although his rhymings can hardly be dignified by the name of poetry, they are certainly not inferior to many of the rhymings of his day and generation.

As before noted, his lines breathe a deep religious feeling and were written with the hope that those who would read them would be led from the ways of sin to righteousness. His poetical address to Miss Wheatley was written with this end in view and may have had more than a passing effect on that young woman.

He was fond of using certain words, and "Salvation" was one of his favorites, it being made use of twenty-three times in his earliest known publication. In this respect he was not unlike the late Bloodgood Cutter, whose favorite word was "did." As a rhymer, however, Hammon far outshines the "Long Island Farmer Poet," who used to boast of his lack of education.

Hammon was also fond of using marginal references from Scripture and in some of his writings they are found at every second line. He was evidently a deep student of the Bible and was inspired by what the Good Book taught him. It seems probable that his effusions were the means of bringing many of his fellow bondmen to the throne of grace.

When we consider that he was probably without any education whatsoever, we marvel that he accomplished as much as he did. Had he had the advantages of learning possessed by Miss Wheatley, it seems possible that as a poet he would have ranked as her equal, if not her superior. His prose writings were also above the mediocre, but from the testimony of one of his printers he was evidently deficient as a speller.

He stands, however, unique in the annals of American Poetry and his works must not be too harshly judged. The disadvantages under which he composed them were probably far greater than we can imagine.

It seems, however, too bad that his verse is entirely of a religious nature. Much would have been added to its interest had he written about some of the events that were transpiring all around him during the War for Independence and the years that followed that struggle.

He seems to have been content to sing the praises of the Master whom he longed to serve and whose reward he some day expected to receive, and with that end in view he labored to instill the blessings of religion into his less fortunate brethren.

For this his memory should be honored and let the broken lines which fell from his pen be cherished, if for no other reason than that they were written by the first American Negro who attempted to give expression to his thoughts in verse.

A VISIT TO HAMMON'S HOME

On the invitation of Mr. Orville B. Ackerly, the best informed student of Long Island history, that gentleman, Mrs. Ackerly and myself motored to Lloyd's Neck on the morning of October 17, last. We were in quest of the last resting place of the poet. Did we find it? No, but the trip was one of the most enjoyable that I have undertaken.

After driving some thirty miles after leaving Jamaica, we arrived at the "Neck," and stopped at the old Lloyd Manor House, now owned by Wm. J. Matheson, and occupied by his daughter, Mrs. W. D. Wood, where we hoped to obtain some information regarding Hammon's grave. The lady, however, was not at home, but one of her employees directed us to the home of one Meyer, a German, who had a reputation of being an authority on the early history of the "Neck." We found him, but as I had expected, he knew nothing about Hammon, but he informed us that the old Lloyd burial plot was no more and that the remains of those interred there had been removed to the Rural Cemetery at Huntington. His daughter, however, directed us to a small burial plot situated in the midst of a dense wood and told us that was where she believed the grave of Hammon might be found. After some search and after wending our way over a path well nigh obliterated with weeds and under-brush, we espied in a little inclosure a few head-stones. How my heart beat high with

23

expectation! At last I was to look upon the last resting place of the old slave-poet. Perhaps the dates of his birth and death were graven thereon; an extract from his poems might even be found cut into the stone?

But no, we were doomed to disappointment, for the plot we had found was the ''God's Acre'' of some of the tenants of Mr. Lloyd. The earliest death noted was that of Thomas Barker who died in 1795 AE. 81.

Mr. Ackerly, who carried his note book with him, made a copy of the inscriptions found on the headstones in the plot, but like myself he is of the opinion that Hammon's remains did not repose there. On our return we stopped once more at the Meyer home, but the old German could not be discovered and a notice on his door informed us that he was ''out in the woods.''

The site of the Lloyd graveyard is now occupied by a neat school house.

Though our trip was without tangible results, it was not altogether useless and I was certainly glad to gaze on the scenes once familiar to the subject of this book, and to ramble through the woods where he was wont to roam, perhaps sitting beneath the shade of some monarch of the forest, mayhap composing beneath the overhanging leaves some of the verses which are to-day his chief claim to fame.

24

HAMMON'S VIEWS ON SLAVERY

The following extracts from "An Address to the Negroes of the State of New York" show plainly that Hammon did not regard slavery as lawful according to the laws of the Creator. He, however, believed it better for his colored brethren to meekly obey their earthly masters as by doing so their condition would be bettered and the hearts of their owners softened thereby. From his own statements he was a favored servant and his life was evidently one of comparative ease. He himself was perfectly content to remain in bondage, but longed to see the younger negroes freed:

"My brethren, when I think of you, which is very often, and of the poor, despised, and miserable state you are in, as to the things of this world; and when I think of your ignorance and stupidity, and the great wickedness of most of you, I am pained to the heart. It is at times, almost too much for human nature to bear; and I am obliged to turn my thoughts from the subject. . . . I have wanted exceedingly to say something to you, to call upon you with the tenderness of a father and friend, and to give you the last, and I may say, dying advice of an old man, who wishes your best good in this world, and in the world to come. But while I have had such desires, a sense of my own ignorance, and unfitness to teach others, has frequently discouraged me from attempting to say anything to you; yet, when I thought of your situation, I could

not rest easy. . . . I think you will be more likely
to listen to what is said, when you know it comes
from a Negro, one of your own Nation and colour; and
therefore can have no interest in deceiving you, or
saying anything to you, but what he really thinks is
your interest and duty to comply with. My age, I
think, gives me some right to speak to you, and reason
to expect you will hearken to my advice. I am now
upwards of seventy years old, and cannot expect,
though I am well and able to do almost any kind of
business, to live much longer. I have passed the com-
mon bounds set for man, and must soon go the way of
all the earth. I have had more experience in the world
than most of you, and I have seen a great deal of the
vanity and wickedness of it. I have had great reason
to be thankful that my lot has been so much better
than most slaves have had. I suppose I have had
more advantages and privileges than most of you, who
are slaves, have ever known and I believe more than
many white people have enjoyed. . . . I do not,
my dear friends, say these things about myself to make
you think that I am wiser and better than others;
but that you might hearken, without prejudice, to what
I have to say to you on the following particulars.

"1st. Respecting obedience to masters. Now,
whether it is right and lawful, in the sight of God, for
them to make slaves of us or not, I am certain that
while we are slaves, it is our duty to obey our masters
in all their lawful commands, and mind them, unless
we are bid to do that which we know to be sin, or for-
bidden in God's word. . . . It may seem hard for us, if
we think our masters wrong in holding us slaves, to
obey in all things! . . . As we depend upon our
masters for what we eat, and drink, and wear, . . .

26

we cannot be happy unless we obey them. Good servants frequently make good masters.

"Now I acknowledge that liberty is a great thing, and worth seeking for, if we can get it honestly; and by our good conduct, prevail on our masters to set us free: though for my own part I do not wish to be free, yet I should be glad if others, especially the young Negroes, were to be free; for many of us who are grown up slaves, and have always had masters to take care of us, should hardly know how to take care of themselves; and it may be more for our own comfort to remain as we are. That liberty is a great thing we may know from our own feelings, and we may likewise judge so from the conduct of the white people in the late war. How much money has been spent, and how many lives have been lost to defend their liberty. I must say that I have hoped that God would open their eyes, when they were so much engaged for liberty, to think of the state of the poor blacks, and to pity us. . . . Let me beg of you, my dear African brethren, to think very little of your bondage in this life; for your thinking of it will do you no good. If God designs to set us free, he will do it in his own time and way; but think of your bondage to sin and Satan, and do not rest until you are delivered from it. . . . I will conclude what I have to say with a few words to those Negroes who have their liberty.

"To most to what I have said to those who are slaves, may be of use to you; but you have more advantages, on some accounts, if you will improve your freedom, as you may do, than they. You have more time to read God's holy word, and to take care of the salvation of your souls.

"One great reason that is given by some for not free-

27

ing us, I understand, is, that we should not know how
to take care of ourselves, and should take to bad
courses; that we should be lazy and idle, and get
drunk and steal.

"Let me beg of you then, for the sake of your own
good and happiness, in time, and for eternity, and for
the sake of your poor brethren, who are still in
bondage. . . ."

He further admonishes them to be honest and
truthful and that his advice was deemed of
value is proved by the fact that the Pennsylvania Society for promoting the abolition of
slavery ordered the book to be reprinted in an
edition of five hundred copies. His plea for the
liberation of the younger negroes seems to have
had an effect on his owner for in his will dated
1795 John Lloyd, Jr., directs that certain of his
negroes, whom he names, should be given their
freedom on reaching the age of twenty-eight.

AN EVENING THOUGHT
SALVATION BY CHRIST, WITH PENETENTIAL CRIES

Salvation comes by Christ alone,
The only Son of God;
Redemption now to every one,
That love his holy Word.
Dear Jesus we would fly to Thee,
And leave off every Sin,
Thy tender Mercy well agree;
Salvation from our King;
Salvation comes now from the Lord,
Our victorious King.
His holy Name be well ador'd,
Salvation surely bring.
Dear Jesus give they Spirit now,
Thy Grace to every Nation,
That han't the Lord to whom we bow,
The Author of Salvation.
Dear Jesus unto Thee we cry,
Give us the Preparation;
Turn not away thy tender Eye;
We seek thy true Salvation.
Salvation comes from God we know,
The true and only One;
It's well agreed and certain true,
He gave his only Son.
Lord hear our penetential Cry:
Salvation from above;
It is the Lord that doth supply,
With his Redeeming Love.
Dear Jesus by thy precious Blood,
The World Redemption have:
Salvation now comes from the Lord,

He being thy captive slave.
Dear Jesus let the Nations cry,
And all the People say,
Salvation comes from Christ on high,
Haste on Tribunal Day.
We cry as Sinners to the Lord,
Salvation to obtain;
It is firmly fixt his holy Word,
Ye shall not cry in vain.
Dear Jesus unto Thee we cry,
And make our Lamentation:
O let our Prayers ascend on high;
We felt thy Salvation.
Lord turn our dark benighted Souls;
Give us a true Motion,
And let the Hearts of all the World,
Make Christ their Salvation.
Ten Thousand Angels cry to Thee,
Yea louder than the Ocean.
Thou art the Lord, we plainly see;
Thou art the true Salvation.
Now is the Day, excepted Time;
The Day of Salvation;
Increase your Faith, do not repine:
Awake ye every Nation.
Lord unto whom now shall we go,
Or seek a safe Abode;
Thou hast the Word Salvation too
The only Son of God.
Ho! every one that hunger hath,
Or pineth after me,
Salvation be thy leading Staff,
To set the Sinner free.
Dear Jesus unto Thee we fly;

Depart, depart from Sin,
Salvation doth at length supply,
The Glory of our King.
Come ye Blessed of the Lord,
Salvation greatly given;
O turn your Hearts, accept the Word,
Your Souls are fit for Heaven.
Dear Jesus we now turn to Thee,
Salvation to obtain;
Our Hearts and Souls do meet **again**,
To magnify thy Name.
Come holy Spirit, Heavenly Dove,
The Object of our Care;
Salvation doth increase our Love;
Our Hearts hath felt thy fear.
Now Glory be to God on High,
Salvation high and low;
And thus the Soul on Christ rely,
To Heaven surely go.
Come Blessed Jesus, Heavenly Dove,
Accept Repentance here;
Salvation give, with tender Love;
Let us with Angels share.   Finis.

AN ADDRESS

TO

MISS PHILLIS WHEATLY

I

O come you pious youth! adore
    The wisdom of thy God,
In bringing thee from distant shore,
    To learn His holy word.

Eccles. xii.

II

Thou mightst been left behind,
    Amidst a dark abode;
God's tender mercy still combin'd,
    Thou hast the holy word.

Psal. cxxxv, 2, 3.

III

Fair wisdom's ways are paths of peace,
    And they that walk therein,
Shall reap the joys that never cease,
    And Christ shall be their king.

Psal. i. 1, 2; Prov. iii, 7.

IV

God's tender mercy brought thee here;
    Tost o'er the raging main;
In Christian faith thou hast a share,
    Worth all the gold of Spain.

Psal. ciii, 1, 3, 4,

32

V

While thousands tossed by the sea,
  And others settled down,
God's tender mercy set thee free,
  From dangers that come down.

Death.

VI

That thou a pattern still might be,
  To youth of Boston town,
The blessed Jesus set thee free,
  From every sinful wound.

2 Cor. v. 10.

VII

The blessed Jesus, who came down,
  Unvail'd his sacred face,
To cleanse the soul of every wound,
  And give repenting grace.

Rom. v, 21.

VIII

That we poor sinners may obtain,
  The pardon of our sin;
Dear blessed Jesus now constrain,
  And bring us flocking in.

Psal. xxxiv, 6, 7, 8.

IX

Come you, Phillis, now aspire,
  And seek the living God,
So step by step thou mayst go higher,
  Till perfect in the word.

Matth. vii, 7, 8.

X

While thousands mov'd to distant shore,
　And others left behind,
The blessed Jesus still adore,
　Implant this in thy mind.

Psal. lxxxix, 1.

XI

Thou hast left the heathen shore;
　Thro' mercy of the Lord,
Among the heathen live no more,
　Come magnify thy God.

Psal. xxxiv, 1, 2, 3.

XII

I pray the living God may be,
　The shepherd of thy soul;
His tender mercies still are free,
　His mysteries to unfold.

Psal. lxxx, 1, 2, 3.

XIII

Thou, Phillis, when thou hunger hast,
　Or pantest for thy God;
Jesus Christ is thy relief,
　Thou hast the holy word.

Psal. xiii, 1, 2, 3.

XIV

The bounteous mercies of the Lord,
　Are hid beyond the sky,
And holy souls that love His word,
　Shall taste them when they die.

Psal. xvi, 10, 11.

XV

These bounteous mercies are from God,
  The merits of His Son;
The humble soul that loves His word,
  He chooses for His own.
Psal. xxxiv, 15.

XVI

Come, dear Phillis, be advis'd,
  To drink Samaria's flood;
There nothing that shall suffice
  But Christ's redeeming blood.
John iv, 13, 14.

XVII

While thousands muse with earthly toys;
  And range about the street,
Dear Phillis, seek for heaven's joys,
  Where we do hope to meet.
Matth. vi, 33.

XVIII

When God shall send his summons down,
  And number saints together,
Blest angels chant, (triumphant sound),
  Come live with me forever.
Psal. cxvi, 15.

XIX

The humble soul shall fly to God,
  And leave the things of time,
Start forth as 'twere at the first word,
  To taste things more divine.
Mat. v, 3, 8.

35

XX

Behold! the soul shall waft away,
  Whene'er we come to die,
And leave its cottage made of clay,
  In twinkling of an eye.

Cor. xv, 51 ; 52, 53

XXI

Now glory be to the Most High,
  United praises given,
By all on earth, incessantly,
  And all the host of heav'n.

Psal. cl, 6.

A POEM FOR CHILDREN WITH THOUGHTS ON DEATH

I

O Ye young and thoughtless youth,
 Come seek the living God,
The scriptures are a sacred truth,
 Ye must believe the word.

Eccle. xii. 1.

II

Tis God alone can make you wise,
 His wisdom's from above,
He fills the soul with sweet supplies
 By his redeeming love.

Prov. iv. 7.

III

Remember youth the time is short,
 Improve the present day
And pray that God may guide your thoughts,
 and teach your lips to pray.

Psalm xxx. 9.

IV

To pray unto the most high God,
 and beg restraining grace,
Then by the power of his word
 You'l see the Saviour's face.

V

Little children they may die,
    Turn to their native dust,
Their souls shall leap beyond the skies,
    And live among the just.

VI

Like little worms they turn and crawl,
    and gasp for every breath.
The blessed Jesus sends his call,
    and takes them to his rest.

VII

Thus the youth are born to die,
    The time is hastening on,
The Blessed Jesus rends the sky,
    and makes his power known.

Psalm ciii. 15.

VIII

Then ye shall hear the angels sing
    The trumpet give a sound,
Glory, glory to our King,
    The Saviour's coming down.

Matt. xxvi. 64.

IX

Start ye saints from dusty beds,
    and hear a Saviour call,
Twas Jesus Christ that died and bled,
    and thus preserv'd thy soul.

X

This the portion of the just,
  Who lov'd to serve the Lord,
Their bodies starting from the dust,
  Shall rest upon their God.

XI

They shall join that holy word,
  That angels constant sing,
Glory, glory to the Lord,
  Hallelujahs to our King.

XII

Thus the Saviour will appear,
  With guards of heavenly host,
Those blessed Saints, shall then declare,
  Tis Father, Son and Holy Ghost.
                              Rev. i. 7, 8.

XIII

Then shall ye hear the trumpet sound,
  The graves give up their dead,
Those blessed saints shall quick awake,
  and leave their dusty beds.
                        Matt. xxvii. 51, 52.

XIV

Then shall you hear the trumpet sound,
  and rend the native sky,
Those bodies starting from the ground,
  In the twinkling of an eye.
                    1 *Cor.* xv. 51, 52, 53, 54.

39

XV

There to sing the praise of God,
and join the angelic train,
And by the power of his word,
Unite together again.

XVI

Where angels stand for to admit
Their souls at the first word,
Cast sceptres down at Jesus feet
Crying holy holy Lord.

XVII

Now glory be unto our God
all praise be justly given,
Ye humble souls that love the Lord
Come seek the joys of Heaven.

HARTFORD, January 1, 1782.

A DIALOGUE INTITLED THE KIND MASTER AND THE DUTIFUL SERVANT AS FOLLOWS:

Composed by JUPITER HAMMON

MASTER.

1. Come my servant, follow me,
        According to thy place;
    And surely God will be with thee,
        And send thee heav'nly grace.

SERVANT.

2. Dear Master, I will follow thee,
        According to thy word,
    And pray that God may be with me,
        And save thee in the Lord.

MASTER.

3. My Servant, lovely is the Lord,
        And blest those servants be,
    That truly love his holy word,
        And thus will follow me.

SERVANT.

4. Dear Master, that's my whole delight,
        Thy pleasure for to do;
    As for grace and truth's in sight,
        Thus far I'll surely go.

5.   My Servant, grace proceeds from God,
      And truth should be with thee;
Whence e'er you find it in his word,
      Thus far come follow me.

SERVANT.

6.   Dear Master, now without controul,
      I quickly follow thee;
And pray that God would bless thy soul,
      His heav'nly place to see.

MASTER.

7.   My Servant, Heaven is high above,
      Yea, higher than the sky:
I pray that God would grant his love,
      Come follow me thereby.

SERVANT.

8.   Dear Master, now I'll follow thee,
      And trust upon the Lord;
The only safety that I see,
      Is Jesus's holy word.

MASTER.

9.   My Servant, follow Jesus now,
      Our great victorious King;
Who governs all both high and low,
      And searches things within.

AN
ADDRESS
TO THE
NEGROES,
IN THE
STATE of NEW-YORK.

By JUPITER HAMMON, Servant of John Lloyd,
jun. Esq. of the Manor of Queen's Village, Long-Island.

" Of a truth I perceive that God is no respecter of persons:
" But in every nation he that feareth him, and worketh righteous-
" ness, is accepted with him."—*Acts* x. 34, 35.

NEW-YORK PRINTED:
PHILADELPHIA RE-PRINTED BY DANIEL HUMPHREYS,
in Spruce-street, near the Drawbridge.
M.DCC.LXXXVII.

10. Dear Master, I will follow thee,
    When praying to our King;
    It is the Lamb I plainly see,
    Invites the sinner in.

MASTER.

11. My Servant, we are sinners all,
    But follow after grace;
    I pray that God would bless thy soul,
    And fill thy heart with grace.

SERVANT.

12. Dear Master I shall follow then,
    The voice of my great King;
    As standing on some distant land,
    Inviting sinners in.

MASTER.

13. My servant we must all appear,
    And follow then our King;
    For sure he'll stand where sinners are,
    To take true converts in.

SERVANT.

14. Dear Master, now if Jesus calls,
    And sends his summons in;
    We'll follow saints and angels all,
    And come unto our King.

15. My servant now come pray to God,
Consider well his call;
Strive to obey his holy word,
That Christ may love us all.

A Line *on the present* war.

SERVANT.

16. Dear Master now it is a time,
A time of great distress;
We'll follow after things divine,
And pray for happiness.

MASTER.

17. Then will the happy day appear.
That virtue shall increase;
Lay up the sword and drop the spear,
And Nations seek for peace.

SERVANT.

18. Then shall we see the happy end,
Tho' still in some distress;
That distant foes shall act like friends,
And leave their wickedness.

MASTER.

19. We pray that God would give us grace,
And make us humble too;
Let ev'ry Nation seek for peace,
And virtue make a show.

20. Then we shall see the happy day,
    That virtue is in power;
Each holy act shall have its sway,
    Extend from shore to shore.

MASTER.

21. This is the work of God's own hand,
    We see by precepts given;
To relieve distress and save the land,
    Must be the pow'r of heav'n.

SERVANT.

22. Now glory be unto our God,
    Let ev'ry nation sing;
Strive to obey his holy word,
    That Christ may take them in.

MASTER.

23. Where endless joys shall never cease,
    Blest Angels constant sing;
The glory of their God increase,
    Hallelujahs to their King.

SERVANT.

24. Thus the Dialogue shall end,
    Strive to obey the word;
When ev'ry Nation acts like friends,
    Shall be the sons of God.

25. Believe me now my Christian friends,
      Believe your friend call'd Hammon:
   You cannot to your God attend,
      And serve the God of Mammon.

26. If God is pleased by his own hand
      To relieve distresses here;
   And grant a peace throughout the the (*sic*) land,
      'Twill be a happy year.

27. 'Tis God alone can give us peace;
      It's not the pow'r of man:
   When virtuous pow'r shall increase,
      'Twill beautify the land.

28. Then shall we rejoice and sing
      By pow'r of virtues word,
   Come sweet Jesus, heav'nly King,
      Thou art the Son of God.

29. When virtue comes in bright array,
      Discovers ev'ry sin;
   We see the dangers of the day,
      And fly unto our King.

30. Now glory be unto our God,
      All praise be justly given;
   Let ev'ry soul obey his word,
      And seek the joy of heav'n.   FINIS.

BIBLIOGRAPHY

An | Evening Thought. | Salvation by Christ, | with | Penetential Cries: | Composed by Jupiter Hammon, a Negro belonging to Mr Lloyd, of Queen's- | Village, on Long-Island, the 25th of December, 1760. | Broadside of 88 lines, printed in double column, and word "Finis" at bottom. Size 10¼x7⅞ inches.

> This broadside proves conclusively that Jupiter Hammon was writing poetry in America at least nine years before Phillis Wheatley published her first work, The Elegy on the Death of Whitefield. It also proves that Hammon was without doubt the first writer of color whose work appeared in print in what is now the United States. The only copy known is in The New York Historical Society. It was probably printed at New York.

Hartford, August 4, 1778. | An Address to Miss Phillis Wheatly, (*sic*) Ethiopian Po- | etess, in Boston, who came from Africa at eight years of age, and | soon became acquainted with the Gospel of Jesus Christ. | (one line, followed by 21 verses of 4 lines each, printed in double column) | Composed by Jupiter Hammon, a Negro Man belonging to Mr. Joseph Lloyd, of Queen's Village, | on Long-Island, now in Hartford. |

> The above lines are published by the Author, and a number of his friends, who desire to join with him in their best | regards to Miss Wheatly. (*sic*) | Broadside, without doubt printed at Hartford. Size 8¾x6 inches. The only known copy is in The Connecticut Historical Society.

An Essay on the Ten Virgins. Composed by Jupiter Hammon, a Negro Man belonging to Mr. Joseph Lloyd of Queen's Village on Long Island, now in Hartford. Hartford: Printed by Hudson and Goodwin, 1779.

> I have been unable to locate a copy of the above. It is mentioned in the Conn. Courant, Dec. 14, 1779. "To be sold at the Printing-Office in Hartford." Although mentioned by several bibliographers, none give a collation and all seem to take their information from the above source, or from Trumbull's list of Conn. imprints. Mr. Trumbull also obtained his information from the advertisement in the *Courant*.

A | Winter Piece: | being a | Serious Exhortation, with a call to the | Unconverted: | and a short | Contemplation | on the | Death of Jesus Christ. | Written by Jupiter Hammon, | A Negro Man belonging to Mr. John Lloyd, of | Queen's Village, on Long Island, now in Hartford. | Published by the Author with the Assistance | of his Friends. | Hartford: | Printed for the Author. | M. DCC. LXXXII: | 8vo. pp. (2), -22, -(1), -24.

> Probably printed by Hudson & Goodwin. "A Poem for children with Thoughts on Death." Occupies pp. (23)-24. Copies are in The Connecticut Historical Society and in The Massachusetts Historical Society Collections. Another is in the Providence Public Library.

An | Evening's Improvement. | Shewing, | the Necessity of beholding | the Lamb of God. | *To which is added,* | A Dialogue, | Entitled, | The Kind Master and | Dutiful Servant. | Written by Jupiter Hammon, a Negro | Man belonging to Mr. *John Lloyd,* of Queen's | Village, on Long-Island, now in Hartford. | Hartford: | *Printed for the Author, by the Assistance of his Friends.* | 8vo. pp. (2), -3-28.

Printed during the Revolution, probably by Hudson & Goodwin. The New York Historical Society has the copy formerly owned by Daniel Parish, Jr. This is the only copy I can trace.

An | Address | to the | Negroes | In the State of New-York, | By Jupiter Hammon, | Servant of John Lloyd, jun, Esq; of the Manor of Queen's Village, Long-Island. | (4 lines from Acts. X. 34, 35.) | New-York: | Printed by Carroll and Patterson | No. 32, Maiden-Lane, | M, DCC, LXXXVII. | 8vo. pp. (2), -III, -IV, -(1), -6-20.

A copy is in the collection of Henry C. Sturges, of New York. Others are in The New York Historical Society and in The John Carter Brown Library.

The Printers of this, the first edition, make the following statement, the wording differing slightly from that in the Philadelphia re-issue:

"As this Address is wrote in a better stile than could be expected from a slave, some may doubt of the genuineness of the Production. The author, as he informs in the

title page, is a servant of Mr. Lloyd, and has been remarkable for his fidelity and abstinence from those vices,
which he warns his brethren against. The manuscript
wrote in his own hand, is in our possession. We have
made no material alterations in it, except in the spelling,
which we found needed considerable correction.

The Printers,
New-York 20*th. Feb.* 1787.

An | Address | to the Negroes, | In The | State
of New-York. | by Jupiter Hammon, Servant of
John Lloyd, | jun. Esq. of the Manor of Queen's
Village, Long-Island. | (3 lines from *Acts*. X.
34, 35. | New-York Printed: | Philadelphia Re-
Printed By Daniel Humphreys, | in Spruce-
Street, near the Drawbridge. | M. DCC. LXXX-
VII. | 8vo. pp. (3),-4-15,-(1).

Dedicated "To the Members of the African Society of
New York." Dated "Queen's Village, 24th. Sept. 1786."
On the last page is the following interesting statement:
"As this address is wrote in a better stile than could be
expected from a slave, some may be ready to doubt of the
genuineness of the production.—The Author, as he informs in the title-page, is a servant of Mr. Lloyd, and
has been remarkable for his fidelity and abstinence from
those vices, which he warns his brethren against. The
manuscript wrote in his own hand, is in the possession
of Messrs. Carroll and Patterson, printers, in New-York.
—They have made no material alterations in it, except
in the spelling, which they found needed considerable
correction. The Printer."
Copies of this edition are in the New York Public
Library, and in the Harvard College Library. A copy in
the New York Historical Society has a leaf preceding
the title which contains the following statement. This
copy is the only one I have been able to trace which has
this leaf.

"At a Meeting of the Acting Committee of the Pennsylvania Society for promoting the Abolition of Slavery, &c. June 30, 1787—A Pamphlet wrote by Jupiter Hammon, servant to John Lloyd, jun. Esq. Queen's Village, Long-Island, and addressed to the African descendants in General, was laid before them. Impressed with a lively sense of the good effects that may result from a re-publication thereof, to those persons to whom it is particularly addressed, Ordered, that Daniel Humphreys be directed to print five hundred copies, for the purposes above mentioned.

Extract from the Minutes.

Thomas Harrison, Clerk
to Acting Committee."

An Address to the Negroes in the State of New York. By Jupiter Hammon. New York: 1806. 12mo. pp. 22.

The compiler of this list had a copy of this edition several years ago. It was printed after Hammon's death and contains an attestation by three residents of Oyster Bay as to the author's good character. Although the latest of the three known editions, it seems to be the most difficult to locate. A copy was in the New York State Library but was destroyed in the fire of 1911.